GUIDING YOUR CHILDREN INTO THEIR DESTINY

Bishop Dr. Godfrey K. Tabansi

ISBN-13: 978-0977861019

Copyright© 2015 Bishop. Dr. Godfrey K. Tabansi. All rights reserved. No part of this book may be used or reproduced in any manner whatsoever without prior permission of the AUTHOR and Divine Publishers Inc except for brief quotations in critical reviews or articles.

Unless otherwise indicated, all scriptures quotations in this book are from the King James Version (KJV) of the Bible

For any information, comments and/or if you would like to reach Bishop Tabansi, please contact us at:

Divine Publishers Inc.
www.divinepublishersinc.com
Email: divinepublishersinc@gmail.com

Guiding Your Children Into Their Destiny

CONTENTS

Acknowledgments — vi

Introduction — vii

Chapter 1 — Pg 1
Our Children, Our Heritage

Chapter 2 — Pg 6
Why Pray Into The Destiny Of Your Children

Chapter 3 — Pg 11
Practical Steps To Actualizing Your Child's Destiny

Chapter 4 — Pg 19
The Value of Building An alter For Your Children

Chapter 5 — Pg 29
Powerful Scripture To Confess Over Your Children

Chapter 6 — Pg 35
Sorting Old Your Children's Foundation

Chapter 7 — Pg 47
Be Encouraged Your Labor Will Be Rewarded

Chapter 8 — Pg 49
Scriptures To Help Parents in Matters Concerning Children

DEDICATION

Lovingly dedicated to the children of the World

ACKNOWLEDGMENTS

I give all the glory and thanks to the Lord God Almighty for the inspiration He gave me to write this little book. I pray that the Holy Spirit would breath new life upon this massage and give it wings to affect the world.

INTRODUCTION

The Bible speaks volumes on parenthood, childcare and the importance of prayers in shaping the destiny of children. For instance, Lamentations 2:19 says, "Arise, cry out in the night: in the beginning of the watches pour out thine heart like water before the face of the Lord: Lift up thy hands toward him for the life of thy young children: that fainte for hunger in the top of every street." That is a direct admonition to us as parents to sit up and begin to pray seriously for our children. The call in that passage is to "cry out in the night." The image that comes to my mind is that of Hannah, Samuel's Mother. With tears streaming down our cheeks we must learn to cry out for our children. This is not a wishy washy kind of prayer. It is not the short devotion before we go to bed. Rather, it is a call to arise 'at the beginning of the watches" to call unto God with weeping for our children. It is a call to travail. God is calling us into deep agonizing and heart-rending travail.

In Proverbs 17:6, it is recorded that "children's children are the crown of old men; and the glory of children are their father" (KJV). Are you determined to be a crowning glory to your children? Shouldn't you begin now to raise a prayer shield over their defenseless heads. Also in Proverbs 20:7; we walketh in his integrity: his children are blessed after him." Don't you realize that you ought to leave a blessing beyond houses, diamonds, gold or silver to your children? A heritage of righteousness is the best legacy you could hope to bequeath to your children. It is of utmost importance that informed parents avail themselves of the resources in the scriptures to help direct the destiny of their children. This is the path of wisdom, and one of the ways we can raise a righteous and dependable generation for the Lord in our time.

The Lord is depending on us to work in partnership with the Holy Spirit to raise a victorious generation for Him, a generation that will repair up the foundations of many generations. "And they that shall be of thee shall build the old waste places; thou shall raise up the foundation of many generations; and thou shall be called, The repairer of the breach, The restorer of paths to dwell in." Isaiah 58:12. That prophecy will not be fulfilled if we fold our hands and relax in our comfort zones. It can only be fulfilled when parents rise up and begin to pray with passion and fervency for their children.

CHAPTER ONE
OUR CHILDREN, OUR HERITAGE

The Bible states without equivocation: LO, children are a heritage of the LORD: and the fruit of the womb is his reward.

As arrows are in the hand of a mighty man; so are children of the youth.

Happy is the man that hath his quiver full of them: they shall not be ashamed but they shall speak with the ashamed; but they shall speak with the enemies in the gate. Ps.127:3-5

A careful reading of that loaded scripture reveals several striking things about the place of children in a home and the larger society.

 1. They are a "heritage of the LORD". This means that children actually come from GOD to increase and extend the life of a family. This is God's way of ensuring that HIS

command to Adam in Genesis 1:27-25 is carried out. Note that your Children are an extension of GOD's Creation on earth. Treat them as such.

2. They are "the fruit of the womb" that depicts the womb as a precious and God given field which is expected to bring forth a fruitful harvest. Is your field barren? You can, through spiritual travail turn your cry and pain in this issue into power. You can hew down that mountain of barrenness. You can break up your "fallow" ground so that the LORD can bless you. See Jeremiah 4:3, I Samuel 1:5-13; Isaiah 54: 1-4; Joel 2:12-14(a).

Therefore also now, Saith the LORD, turn ye even to me with all your heart, and with weeping, and with mourning:

And rend your heart, and not your garments; and turn unto the LORD your GOD: for he is gracious and merciful

3. They are a "reward' from the LORD for services God only can evaluate. What kind of reward do you want your children to bring you? You can actually begin to influence the kind of life they should live right from when they are still in the womb.

4. With proper grooming and the right kind of training they could serve in the kind of a "mighty man" as sharp "arrows". The "mighty man" referred to in Psalm 127:4 is an allusion to a disciplined father who is skilled in using the woman of God; a spiritual warrior and a man of substance who is wise enough to inspire in the training of his

children. You owe God a responsibility to train your children. In fact, training your children is a direct command from God. The Bible says, "Train up a child in the way he should go: and when he is old, he will not depart from it", Proverbs 22:6. Of Abraham God testified saying "for I know him, that he will command his children and his household after him and they shall keep the way of the LORD to do justice and judgment; that the LORD may bring upon Abraham that which he hath spoken of him". Gen. 18:19. Joshua, the great Leader who took over from Moses said to the Camp of Isreal:"…..but as far me and my house, we will serve the LORD" Joshua 24:15(d)

5. Your children grow to become your companions when you have them in your youth.

6. Children bring joy and happiness to a home. The couples who have them are adjudged happy, favored, blessed and fruitful. A couple without children can sometimes experience real sadness and pain. Rachel cried out in her bareness "give me a child or I die" read Genesis 15:1-2, 16:12, 25: 20-21, 30:1-3, to find out how the couples mentioned in these scripture passages coped with temporary bareness.

7. Parents who bring up their children properly are not ashamed when the day of reckoning comes: Proverbs 25: 24-25; 29:15. What does this involve? It involves making out quality time to sit down and talk loving to your children. Play with them and curdle them. Eat with them and take them out for sightseeing. Censor the things they watch on television, spend time to watch the cartoons that your children are so engrossed in. Listen to the kind of music they listen to and look into the background of their

friends they keep and get to know them; invite these friends to your house. Find out what your children are getting involved in as they surf the internet. This would be your only clue about the source of the strange behavior of your teenage son or daughter. It could be the early warning signals to save your children from initiation into witchcraft, Cults, gangs and drugs.

8. In the event of an attack against a man and his home, his children, "the arrows in his quiver", join hands with him to defend their turf, they fight as a formidable team. Abraham single handedly raised 318 good fighters in his own home. He trained them to be good warriors. See Genesis 14:14-16.

In view of these things we have said, what manner of parents should we be? Should we not dim to be righteous and submitted to God so that we maybe able to give our children the right counsel? Should we not explore ways to ensure that our homes are established in righteousness and our children preserved? The Bible says, "the house of the wicked shall be over thrown but the tabernacle of the upright shall flourish". Proverbs 14:11

Praying into the destiny of your children, training them in the fear of the Lord and modeling the Christian Life to them will help disentangle your children from Satan's web. We have a great responsibility not only to instruct but to pray fervently for our children to escape Satan's snares in his perverse and corrupt generation

CHILDCARE:

1. The issue of childcare should be handled properly.

2. Mothers are answerable to God for the way they treat their children.

3. Some mothers give no proper training to their children nor pay any special attention to their Children.

4. Children are left in the hands of cruel nannies and/or babysitters who influence their lives with cruelty.

5. Child care must be seriously looked into.

6. What training do mothers give to their children?

7. What values or virtues do they import?

8. Do not leave your children with just anyone.

9. Proper care should be taken concerning the grooming of children.

10. Let their lives be influenced positively.

CHAPTER TWO

WHY PRAY INTO THE DESTINY OF YOUR CHILDREN

There are several reasons why we must make a concrete decision to pray for our children. We must pray for their protection, for the favor of God upon their lives and for their destiny to be fulfilled. The Bible promises help to all parents when they call upon God for their children in the days of trouble.

"Call unto me, and I will answer thee, and shew thee great and mighty things, which thou knowest not" Jer.: 33-3

Each child has a destiny to fulfill and a place to exercise dominion in God in this world. Without prayer these destinies may not be fulfilled. We really do not know our children or what they are meant to be in God's hands. That is why we have to pray. Below are some suggestions on how to pray for our Children.

1. Pray for their health. The children need good health. Pray that their health will spring forth like the morning.

This is God's will for your children. "Beloved I wish above all things that thou mayest prosper and be in (good) health, even as they soul prospereth" 3 John 1:2. If the children are not alive and healthy they can't fulfill their destiny.

2. Pray that our children's ways will be ordered by the LORD. The scripture says that the steps of a righteous man are ordered by the LORD. When children veer off into sin they cannot be blessed or protected. Lead your children to pray this prayer daily: "Shew me thy ways, O' LORD: Teach me thy paths. Lead me in thy truth, and teach me: For thou are the God of my salvation, on thee do I wait all the day" . Psalms 25:4-5

3. Using III John verse eleven as a reference, Cut them off from peer pressure. The peer groups has such a powerful influence on children that they could drawn away from the right way – if the parents do not take steps to arrest the situation. Ask the LORD to lead your children in the path of everlasting. Psalm 139:24(b)

4. Pray that God's spirits will stabilize them to walk right and live right in this troubled generation.

5. Using Daniel 1:17-20, ask God to cause your children to be wise and to be ten times better than their peers. Pray that they will excel in their academics, prophesize that they will be on top and not beneath. Declare that your children will be the head and not the tail.

6. Pray that they will not suffer frustration in their school assignments or examinations. Pray that your children will walk in integrity and God's truth. Ask that

wherever God places them they will demand justice and equity for all. Pray that your children will be bold as lions. 'Let integrity and uprightness preserve me: For I want on thee". Psalms 25-21

7. Cancel Satan's assignments over your children's lives. He comes to steal, to kill and destroy. Cancel Satan's mission to attach a strange child as an agent to pullute and defile the pure seed in your children. (Mal. 2:15). Begin to pray for your children's marriages right after they are born. Even if it takes 30 or more years, keep praying to water the ground for their success. That way they can never go wrong in making the right choices. Your fervent prayers will ensure that each one of your children finds a spouse after God's heart.

8. Speak into the dream or talent that God has given to your child. In the Name of Jesus, speak to the dream in God's heart for your child. Declare to the whole of creation saying release your sweet influences to fertilize my child's dream. "O hosts of heaven, fight in your courses against any force that comes to destroy my child's talent in Jesus name." Please realize that Satan is targeting the children. Why? Because this is the generation that should reap the harvest for God. Satan is mad at them. Jeremiah 31:15-17 shows that you can "weep with bitter lamentation before God for your children" When they begin to go astry. Verse 17 shows that there is hope and that your children shall return....(Jeremiah 31:17).

When a child starts going astry it shows he is disconnected from God. When your child starts using drugs such as smoking Indian Hemp or Cannabis,

Crack and sniffing cocaine, it shows he is without roots and does not know where he is going. In the world today Satan has ensured the souls of many students in higher institutions through cultism and blood covenants. Even if this happens to one of your children, don't become so discouraged that you can not pray. Cry out to God for these young lives. Never give up on your children because God has need of them; God needs them because of the big dreams He has put in them. God needs big dreamers. God needs this generation to gather in the harvest. The field is white and the laborers are so few. Move now, fall on your knees and begin to pray for your children.

As you pray, ask the LORD to put a huge dream in the hearts of all the millions of disconnected, deceived and misled young people in the world. Ask God to put a powerful dream in their heart: Such as He put in Joseph's heart.

9. Call forth restoration of families. Ask the Lord to restore the years that the canker worm and the caterpillar have destroyed in the lives of families where children have rebelled from parental authority and from God's commands. Call forth the Joshua generation to rise up. Pray for Ministers and their children who have drifted from the LORD and are running away from the path of truth. Pray that God will bring them back and heal their broken relationships.

10. Pray for the orphans, street children and children from broken homes. These ones have no one to love and care for them. They need Christ's healing touch. They need your love and prayers. They need to be

evangelized and "harvested" into the Kingdom. I am appalled at the degree of poverty and deprivation of street children of Africa and the world over. Pray for several thousands of Children all over the world orphaned by AIDS. They need your prayers and goodwill; they need your love and prayers. They need Christ's healing touch. They need to be evangelized and "harvested" into the kingdom.

11. Pray for drug Addicts. These include young people who are doing drugs. Their lives are being slowly destroyed by cocaine, and all kinds of hard drugs. Ask God to help them kick the habit and heal them completely. Ask God to save them and their parents/care takers. Ask the LORD to bring restoration to their lives.

12. Pray for children caught in the caldron of hatred and War. Ask God to break touch their hearts.

CHAPTER 3

PRACTICAL STEPS TO ACTUALIZING YOUR CHILD'S DESTINY

NAMING YOUR CHILD

In unveiling the secrets of praying into the destiny of your children, let us begin with the very names you give them.

1. Ask from the Lord the name of your child even before he/she is born. Don't allow your parents to give your children useless and meaningless names. This is important because the name defines the nature and mission of the child. It reveals his or her work. Abigail, the wise woman, while pleading for Nabal(her foolish husband) said to David, please forgive him, "...for as his name is so is he; Nabal is his name, and folly is with him..." 1 Samuel 25:25, In describing Nabal the Bible says "... the man was childish and evil in his doing"(1 Samuel 25:3). By inference, we can say that Nabal acted out the meaning of the name he bore. This is why we should give our children good names. When God gives you a name and call forth the destiny embedded in the name. by doing so the child

will be established and blessed. He will be empowered to fulfill his mission on earth.

2. Celebrate each child right from the womb. Love the child. Pray for the child very specifically. Talk to the child. Address your unborn child with Psalms and hymns and very powerful scriptures. The fetus can hear you. It has been scientifically proven that the things happen to a woman during pregnancy do affect the child she bears. If you are happy, the child will be happy. If you sing often, and you dance and worship the LORD, the child will learn from you. If you play some musical instruments of dance often, the child responds while still in the womb. Children can hear and respond to the things you say. John the Baptist leaped in his mother's womb when Mary, the mother of Jesus greeted Elizabeth her cousin. This encounter is recorded in Luke 1:41. This passage illustrates that some children can actually be filled with the Holy Spirit right from the womb. So it is not out of place to ask the Holy Spirit to brood over your child daily to help order his or her life aright. Bless the child, and prophesize into the child's future.

3. Build an alter for your child. Hannah did this for Samuel: 1 Samuel 1:22-28. Celebrate every child's birthday meaningfully by raising an alter for the child. A good way to begin the celebration is to thank and bless the LORD for the life of your child. If the child's birthday falls on a Sunday of your fellowship/Church meeting day, it is perfectly in order to take that child to the church and ask your Pastor/Elders to pray and prophesize over the child.

They could also rededicate and anoint the child, Praising God, Worshipping him, making proclamations into your child's birthday and praying to order the times and seasons of his/her life are some of the things you could do privately before inviting friends and relatives to share in the joy of the celebration. Whether you bake the cake or cook a large meal to celebrate the child's birthday is immaterial. The important thing is that you deliberately bless the child and prophesize over his/her life. Abraham made a large feast to celebrate Isaac. Genesis 21:1-8. Friends and neighbors were invited and there was plenty to eat for every guest who came. There was laughter and merriment in Abraham's household on account of Isaac's birth. Sarah his mother said, "The LORD has made me to laugh so that all that hear it will laugh with me"(Genesis 21:6). Let the birth of your child bring joy to your home. Hannah wrote a powerful prophetic song to celebrate Samuel. 1 Samuel 2:1-10. Dedicate your child by placing him/her in God's hands for safe keeping. Jesus was dedicated on the 8th Day. Simeon the devout man and Anna the prophetess blessed the child Jesus. Read the details in Luke 2: 25-38.

4. Protect the candle of your Child's life. Proverbs 28:27 says "The spirit of man is the candle of the LORD, searching all the inward parts of the belly." And in Psalm 18:28 we read, "For thou with light my candle: the LORD my God will enlighten my darkness." Be wise don't terminate your child's life midstream or frustrate his or her progress. Don't allow just anybody lay hands on your chil birthday candle. This is because the candle is a symbol of your child's light and its brightness. It is only the candle of the wicked that God puts out. In two chapters in the book

of –Job we read:

> a. How often is the candle of the wicked put out! And how often cometh their destruction upon them! God distributh sorrows in his anger. Job 21:17
>
> b. Yea the light of the wicked shall be put out, and the spark of his fire shall not shine.
>
> c. The light shall be dark in his tabernacle, and his candle shall be put out with him Job 18:5-6.

Many people get carried away by the fanfare at birthday parties and follow ignorantly the tradition of blowing off the candle. Please from now on, don't do anything without careful reflection. Did you ever ask yourself why the candle must be blown out? The candle represents your child's light, his life span and glory. Allow that candle to burn out. You can actually teach your children using the candle. But please don't make that candle an idol. Don't worship it. Only let it burn slowly till it goes out by itself. Let the child's life run its full course. Always dedicate the child to God every birthday.

5. Charge Creation to favor your child/Children. Address the heavens and the earth, charging the whole of creation to favor your child/children and release sweet fragrances d. And please don't allow either the child's or his upon him or her. Charge the sun not to smite him/her. Charge the moon and the stars to bless your child/children. Speak to the earth, the winds and waves to help your child. Make

clear proclamations into your child's birthday and order his/her life well. God asked Job a very revealing question: "hast thou commanded the morning since thy days and caused the dayspring to know of the ends of the earth, that the wicked might be shaken ot of it?" Job 38: 12-13. Learn from the challenge God placed before Job

6. Ask God for the purpose of your child's life and also ask HIM the purpose for which the LORD created your child. Psalm 139:14-16, Jeremiah 1:5, Acts 9: 15-16

7. Call forth his/her star. Pray calling forth your child's star to shine brightly. Ask the LORD to increase your child's greatness on every side. "Thou shall increase my greatness, and comfort on every side." Psalm 71:2. Realize that every child has a star. In Genesis 15:5 God said to Abraham even when he had no child yet: ".....Look now toward heaven and tell the stars, if thou be able to number them: and he said unto him so shall they seed be." God compared the off springs of Abraham to the stars of heaven. We know of the star that announced Jesus's birth to the wise men (Mathew 2:2). The eleven stars of Joseph brothers bowed to Joseph's Star. (Genesis 37:9) Pray removing every covering cast or limitation over your child's star.

8. Make room for your children. Pray and ask God to bring your children into their own place, the particular throne from which they are destined to exercise dominion over the earth. Pray I Chronicles 4:10 for your children.

We all need enlarged Coasts.

9. Proverbs 18:16 shows that a man's gift makes room for him, and brings him before great men. Begin now to identify the talent that God has graciously given to your children. Pray over this talent and call it forth. Ask God to help your children use their talents to the best of their ability. Pray that your children will be brought the great men in their generation because of the gifting in their lives. Call forth the Bezaleef anointing and the spirit of excellence which made Daniel great to rest upon your children.

10. Pray and ask the LORD to light the candle of each child's life. Psalm 18:28 which we have referred to earlier shows that God does light the candle of our lives; we need the Holy Spirit to enlighten our darkness. "For thou will light my candle: the LORD my God will enlighten my darkness.

11. Pray and ask the LORD to help your children fulfill their days and leave a blessing to the next generation. Each one of us has to properly hand over the baton of ministry in the particular area to which we have been called to serve, to those who will succeed us.

12. Pray, consecrate your children, their talents, and gifting totally, unreservedly to his service. Bear in mind that their times are in God's hands. Psalm 31:15 states; "My times are in thy hands: deliver me from the hand of mine enemies, and from them that persecute me".

Someone has observed that time is life and that life is very short.

David said in Psalm 89:47(a) "Remember how short my time is...."

13. Pray that God will deliver your children from the hands/plots of the enemy of their Soul. Psalm 144: 7-8; Psalm 71: 4-5; Psalm 34:7 "The angle of the LORD encompeth round about that fear him, and delivereth them'.

14. Pray that God will deliver your children from procrastination which is the thief of time.

15. Pray and ask the LORD to search their hearts, cleanse them from sin and establish them in the path of truth and understanding. Psalm 139:23-24.

16. Pray and ask the LORD to help them walk with him in wisdom. Psalm 27:11 "Teach me thy way, O LORD, and lead me in a plain path, because of my enemies".

17. Proverbs 22:15 says, "Foolishness is bound in the heart of a child, but the rod of correction shall drive if far from him". Therefore as you pray for your children you must be ready to also discipline them with the "rod of correction". If you do a proper job of instructing, correcting and disciplining your children at the right time, you will experience joy and gladness when they mature as adults. These scriptures shows that this is the proper thing to do.

Proverbs 13:24: He that spareth rod hateth his son: But he that loveth him chasteneth him betimes.

Proverbs 23:24: The father of the righteous shall greatly rejoice: and he that begetheth a wise child shall have – Joy of him.

Proverbs 23-25: Thy father and they mother shall be glad, and that bare thee shall rejoice.

Proverbs 29:25: "The rod and reproof give Wisdom: But a child left to himself bringeth his mother to shame.

Proverbs 29:17: "Correct the son, and he shall give thee rest: yea, he shall give delight unto thy soul".

CHAPTER 4

THE VALUE OF BUILDING AN ALTER FOR YOUR CHILDREN

There is value in seeking God's face for your children. Job, the righteous man did this continually for his children. He built an alter to pray for and consecrate his children. He offered burnt offerings to ask God to forgive their sins and keep them pure from the defilement of the world.

And it was so, when the days of their feasting were gone about, that job sent and sanctified them, and rose up early in the morning, and offered burnt offerings according to the number of them all for Job said, it may be that my sons have sinned, and cursed God in their hearts. Thus did Job continually Job 1:5. We should emulate Jobs example. God answers prayers and He will surely answer our prayers for our children.

Apart from asking for protection and pleading with God to forgive your children's sins, you can make enquiries about their lives at the alter. Inquire about the child's destiny and prepare him/her to actualize the destiny. Every mother must pray and ask God to show her the destiny of her child. Only when we know God's purpose for sending the child into this world will we adequately prepare him/her for life and for service in God's Kingdom. Beginning from Genesis, parents, especially mothers, were taking into confidence and permitted to have a glimpse of the destiny of their children. I made an interesting discovery as I studied the scriptures I am about to share with you. In each family it was the parent who had a close encounter relationship with God who had this revelation. A few examples will serve to illustrate this point.

1. Abraham knew the future of Ishmael and Isaac. He was shown what each of his boys would become. (Genesis 21:10-13). 1. Genesis 17:15-19, Genesis 22:1-1 The LORD Almighty made Abraham know that although he would enrich Ishmael and make him the progenitor of a great nation, the inheritance and God's promise concerning Ishmael would come through Isaac. That is why the LORD directed Abraham to cast out Hagar the bond woman and her son,, Ishmael. Genesis 21:12-13. "And God said unto Abraham, let it not be grievous in thy sight because of the lad, and because of thy bondwoman; in all that Sarah hath said unto thee, hearken unto her voice; for in Isaac shall thy see be Called". And also of the son of the bondwoman will I make a nation, Because he is thy seed."

"And as for Ishmael, I have heard thee: Behold, I have blessed him, and will make him, fruitful and will multiply him exceedingly twelve princes shall he beget, and I will make him a great nation." (Genesis 17:20 – emphasis mine).

Hagar, Ishmael's mother, had a preview of who her son would be. She had lengthy conversation with the angel of the LORD at the well called Beer – La-hai-roi where she was shown the water fountain to quench her thirst and save her son from dying. See Genesis 16:7-16

2.   Rebecca knew that Jacob would be greater than Esau. Genesis 25:21-26. Unfortunately she thought she could make God speed up the process by teaching Jacob to Cheat. Rebecca plotted Jacob's act of deception which secured for the younger son the blessing that Isaac planned to give to Esau. Genesis 27:5-38. This was wrong and the lesson is that we must not teach our children to sin. Why? Because only righteousness can exact people. Sin will always bring reproach. "Righteousness exalteth a nation: but sin is a reproach to any people." Proverbs 14:34

3.   Jacob knew by divine revelation that Joseph's younger son (Ephraim) would be greater than Manasseh, the first born. Genesis 48:9-20. It was divine wisdom and prophetic insight that made Jacob set Ephtaim before Manasseh. This is supported by God's declaration in Jeremiah 31:9c "… for I am a Father to Israel and Ephraim is my first born."

4.   Jacob also pronounced specific blessings upon his children because he knew their Destiny by leading of the Holy Spirit. Read Genesis 49: 1-28 to find out how you too can learn to pray blessing into your children's lives

5.   Jacobed, the mother of Moses, knew by divine revelation that Moses was a special child. "And the woman conceived, and bare a son: and when she saw him that he was a goodly Child, she had him three months" Exodus 2:2. That was why she took the risk to preserve his life. The realization that Moses has a critical role to play in the destiny of the Jews in Egypt emboldened Jecobed to come forward to nurse him at Pharaoh's Court, after pharaoh's daughter had picked him from the bulrushes on the River Nile Exodus 2:3-10.

6.   Manoah's wife was visited by an angel, who was sent to reveal the identity and mission of the child she was to bear., Judges 13:3-21. Interestingly, when Manaoh thought that he and his wife would die because they had talked face to face with the "Angle of the LORD", His wife recognized that God had no intention of harming them because they were special instruments in God's hands to bring to pass the Angel's message concerning Samson's destiny. Judges 13:22-23; proves very convincingly that only those who have an intimate relationship with God can know it is mind on any revealed issue. "And Manoah said unto his wife, we shall surely die, because we have seen God. "But his wife said unto him, if the LORD were pleased to kill us he would not have received a burnt offering and a meat offering at our hands, neither would he have shewed us all these things, nor would at this time have told us such things as those."

7.   Zacharias, the Father of John the Baptist, knew who John would be. Luke I: 60-80. The great prophet who came in the spirit of Elijah was such a critical factor in the revelation of God's plans concerning Jesus Chirst, that his

parents were given very strick instruction on how to bring him up. See Luke 1: 13-17.

8.   Mary the mother of Jesus also knew who Jesus was even before He was born. Luke 1:26-35. The Bible says she kept all that the Angel told her, pondering over the awesome responsibility that God had placed upon her and yielding herself totally to his will. "And Mary said, Behold the handmaid of the Lord; be it unto me according to thy word. And the angel departed from her." Luke 1:38.
As Mary meditated upon the things the angel had told her, she received inspiration to sing God's praise in what has become known as the "Magnificat."

"...My soul doth magnify the Lord, and my spirit hath rejoiced in God my Salvation.
For he hath regarded the low estate of his handmaiden: for, behold, from henceforth
all generation shall call me blessed.
For he that is might hath done to me great things; and holy is his name.
And his mercy is on them that fear him from generation to generation.
He hath shewed strength with his arm; he hath scathered the proud in the imagination
of their hearts.
He hath put down the mighty from their seats, and exalted them of low degree. He
hath filled the hungry with good things; and the rich he hath sent empty away.
He hath holpen his servant Israel, in remembrance of his mercy: As he spoke to our fathers, to Abraham, and to his seed forever."
Luke 1:46-55

If you meditate carefully on this poetic song of

thanksgiving and praise to God you will see the greatness of God in revealing himself to a mere mortal who was divinely chosen to carry out his plans. You'll see also that God chooses ordinary women like Mary as vessels to bear precious seed for him. When he chooses any vessel for His works he also empowers that vessel to do the assignment. Therefore we need to constantly pray for the infilling of the Holy Spirit. Mary had this benefit. She was overshadowed by the Holy Spirit before she became pregnant with the Holy Ghost. Luke 1:43-45. Otherwise how on earth could Mary, the young country girl from Nazareth, have known all the prophetic words that she sang in the above quoted passage?

Even more mysterious, how on earth did Elizabeth(an elderly wife of a priest who presumably did not do public ministry herself) Suddenly became bold enough to speak too Mary the words of the canticles? Said Elizabeth to Mary, "… Blessed art thou among women, and blessed is fruit of thy womb."

And whence is this to me that the mother of my Lord should come to me.

For, Lo, as soon as the voice of the salutation sounded in my ears, the babe leaped in my womb for joy. And blessed is she that believed: for there shall be a performance of those things which were told her from the Lord."Luke 1:42-45.
Note that the Bible says Elizabeth spoke to Mary "in a Loud Voice." That was not her normal way of speaking. It was unnatural for women in that part of the world to speak with such a loud voice. It took the Holy Spirit working in their lives of these ordinary women to bring forth such

powerful prophetic utterances.

9. Eunice and Lois, Timothy's mother and grandmother prayed God's will into the life of the young man. We don't know much about Timothy's father who was Greek, but we know that Eunice his mother was a Jewess. Acts 16:1. With the help of Lois, Eunice "trained up" Timothy "in the way he should go" and when he grew older he "did not depart from it". This is what Proverb 22:6 teaches.
And little wonder that God used Timothy so mightily as an assistant to Paul the Apostle, Pray Psalm 90:12 into your children's lives. Ask God daily to teach them how to number their days so that they may apply their hearts to wisdom.

10. Teach your children to fear and reverence the LORD. Why? Because the fear of the LORD is the beginning of wisdom. And wisdom is the principal thing we need to live useful lives on this planet. "This fear of the LORD is the beginning of knowledge.

11. Pray that your Children will grow p as green olive trees in the house of God. "But I am like a green olive tree in the house of God: I trust the mercy of God for ever and ever Psalm 52:8.

12. Pray also that they will be useful in God's House. Ps. 144:12: "that our sons may be as plants grown up in their youth: that our daughters may be as corner stones, polished after the similitude of a palace".
Pray that your Children will grow up as green olive trees in the house of God. "But I am like a green olive tree in the house of God: I trust the mercy of God forever and ever Psalm 52:8 . Pray also that they will be useful in God's

house. Ps. 144:12: "that our sons may be as plants grown up in their youth: that our daughters may be as corner stones, polished after the similitude of a palace.

13. Pray that God will order the steps of your children to do righteousness all the days of their lives. Psalm 37:23, Job 29;14

14. Ask the Lord to deliver your children from the striving of men's tongues and from the hands of the wicked. Ps. 71:4-5 is a good scripture to confess daily over your children. "Deliver my children, O my God out of the hand of the wicked, out of the unrighteous and cruel man."

15. Ask God to prepare a table of fat things for your children in the presence of their enemies. Psalm 23:5. From Ps 128:3(b). Pray that "your children shall surround your table like olive plants."

16. Pray that God would separate your children from the company of strange children. "Rid(my children), and deliver(them) from the hand of strange children, whose mouth speaketh vanity, and their right hand is a right hand of falsehood" Psalm 144:11

17. Pray that your children will grow up to become honorable men. Ask also, that God would enlarge their coasts. "Thou hast enlarge my steps under me that my feet did not slip." Ps. 18:36. And Jabez was more honorable than his brethren; and his mother called his name Jabez saying because I bare him with sorrow. And Jabez called on the God of Israel, saying, Oh that thou would bless me indeed, and enlarge my coast, and that thine hand might be with me, and that thou wouldest keep me from exit, that it

may not grieve me! And God granted him that which he requested. 1chr. 4:9-10.

18. Pray that the ears that hear your children would bless them and the eyes that see them should esteem them. Job. 29:11

19. Pray that God would grant your children great favor. That their steps would be washed in butter and every rock they step on will pour out rivers of oil to bless them. Job 29:6

20. Pray that in this upside-down-world God would make your children serve as a viable extension of his hands to heal the sick, raise the dead and bring success to those in distress. Ask that the Lord would make your children "eyes to the blind and feet to the lame." Job 29:15

21. Fast for your children. In Ezra 8:21 we read these powerful words "then I proclaimed a fast there, at the river of Ahava, that we might afflict ourselves before our God, to seek of him a right way for us, and for our little ones, and for us, and for our little ones, and for all our substance." When we become so burdened about the way our children live and the things they do that we set aside a day or period to fast and pray for them. God will certainly hear us. We must seek a "right way for our children." We can do this most effectively when we fast and pray. Cry about spare not, lift up thy voice like a trumpet, and show my people their transgression, and the house of Jacob their sins. Isaiah 58:1
Is it such a fast that I have chosen? A day for a man to afflict his soul? Is it to bow down his head as a bulrush,

and to spread sachcloth and ashes under him? Wilt thou call this a fast, and acceptable day to the LORD?

Is not this the fast that I have chosen? To loose the hands of wickedness, to undo the heavy burdens, and to let the oppressed go free, and that ye break every yoke? Isiah 58: 5-6

CHAPTER 5

POWERFUL SCRIPTURES TO CONFESS OVER YOUR CHILDREN

Joshua 1:8 says:
This book of the law shall not depart out of the mouth: but thou shall meditate therein day and night, that thou mayest observe to do according to all that is written therein: for then thou shalt make thy way prosperous, and then thou shalt have good success.

And David, the sweet Psalmist of Isreal said: Thy word have I hid in mine heart, that I might not sin against thee Ps 119:11

Thy word is a lamp unto my feet and a light unto my path Ps 119:105

Teach your children as soon as they learn to speak to confess scriptures that can build them up. Here, I will share with you a few of my favorite passages. As you may insert your children's names in the scripture passages and claim the promise contained in them for your children.

Even better teach them to personalize the rich promises contained in the scriptures.

Isaiah 60:1: Arise, shine; for thy light is come, and the glory of the LORD is risen upon the.

Job 33:4: The spirit of God hath made me, and the breath of the Almighty hath given light

Psalm 5:7: But as for me, I will come unto thy house in the multitude of thy house in the multitude of thy mercy: and in the fear will I worship toward thy holy temple.

Psalm 17:8 Keep me as the apple of your eye, hide me under the shadow of thy wings.

Psalm 118:19: Open to me the gates of righteousness; I will go unto them and I will praise the LORD.

Psalm 118:20: This gate of the LORD, into which the righteous shall enter.

Psalm 118:21: I will praise thee for thou host heard me, and art become my salvation.

Psalm 119:15: I will meditate in thy precepts, and have respect unto thy ways.

Psalm 119:16: I will delight myself, myself in thy statutes; I will not forget thy word.

Psalm 119:17: Deal Bountifully with thy servant, that I may live, and keep thy word.

Psalm 119:18: Open thou my eyes, that I may behold wonderous things out of thy law

Psalm 18:32: it is God's that girdeth me with strength.

Psalm 5:8: Lead me, O LORD, in thy righteousness because of my enemies; make thy way straight before my face.

Isiah 49:8: Thus saith the LORD, In an acceptable time have I have heard thee, and in a day of salvation have I helped thee: and give thee for a covenant of the people, to establish the earth, to cause to inherit the desolate heritages.

Isaiah 49:16 Behold, I have graven thee upon the palms of my hands, thy walls are continually before me.

Psalms 5:12: for thou, LORD will bless the righteous: with favor wilt thou compass him as with a shield.

Palms 17:5: Hold up my goings in thy paths, that my footsteps slip not.

Psalms 17:6: I have called upon thee, for thou wilt hear me, O God: Incline thine ear unto me, and hear my speech.

Psalms 17:7: Shew thy marvelous loving kindness, O thou that savest by the right hand them which put their trust in thee from those that rise up against them, and maketh my way perfect.

Psalms 18:33: He maketh my feet like hinds feet and setheh me upon my high places.

Psalms 19:13: Keep back thy servant also from presumptuous sins; let them not have dominion over me; then shall I be upright and I shall be innocent from the great transgression

Psalms 19:14: Let the words of my mouth, and the meditation of my heart, be acceptable in thy sight, O LORD, my strength, and my Redeemer.

Psalms 27:4: One thing have I desired of the LORD, that will I seek after, that I may dwell in the house of the LORD all the days of my life, to behold of the beauty of the LORD, and to enquire in his temple.

Psalms 30:11: Thou hast turned for me my mourning into dancing: thou has put off my sackcloth, and girded me with gladness:

Psalms 30:12: To the end that my glory may sing praise to the, and not be silent: O LORD my God, I will give thanks unto thee forever.

Psalms 31:15: My times are in thy hand: deliver me from thy hand of my enemies, and from them that persecute me.

Psalms 31:21: Blessed be the LORD: For he hath shewed me his marvelous kindness in a strong city.

Psalms 141:1: LORD, I cry unto thee: Make haste unto me; give ear unto my voice, when I cry unto thee

Psalms 141:2: Let my prayer be set forth before thee as incense; and the lifting up of my hands as the evening sacrifice.

Psalms 139:14: I will praise thee, for I am fearfully and wonderfully made: Marvelous are thy works....

Psalms 139:15: My substance was not hid from thee, when I was made in secret, and curiously wrought in the parts of the earth.

Psalms 139:16: Thine eyes did see my substance, yet being unperfect; and in thy book all my members were written, which in continuance were fashioned, when as yet there was none of them.

Psalms 92:10: But my horn shall thou exalt like the horn of an unicorn; I shall be anointed with fresh oil.

Psalms 71:21: Thou shalt increase my greatness, and comfort me on every side.

Psalms 139:23: Search me; O God, and know my heart; try me, and know my thought.

Psalms 139-24: and see if there be any wicked way in me, and lead me in the way everlastings.

Psalms 138:8: The LORD will perfect that which concerneth me; thy mercy, O LORD, endureth for ever: Forsake not the works of thine own hands.

ECCL: 12:1 I remember now thy creator in the days of thy youth, while the exil days come not, not the years when thou shall say, I have no pleasure in them.

ECCl: 12:13: let hear the conclusions of the whole matter; fear God, and keep his commandments; for this is the whole duty of man.

Proverbs 4:20: My son, attend to my words; incline thine ear unto my sayings.

Proverbs 4:21: let them not depart from thine eyes; keep them in the midst of thine heart.

CHAPTER 6

SORTING OUT YOUR CHILDREN'S FOUNDATION

Psalms 11:3 is a scripture all parents must pay particular attention to. It declares "if the foundation be destroyed what can the righteous do?" This is a critical question we all have to answer because the foundation determines a lot of things that happen to an individual or family if some of us had parents who knew what to do about our evil foundations we probably would not have experienced some of the ugly things we have seen. Genesis 38:1-30 shows that the immoral sin Judah affected his descendants for ten generations.

David's sin also affected his descendants. His son Amnon raped his daughter, Tamar and this led to murder in the family.(see 2 Samuel 11:2-5). The sins of the father do affect their children but this ought not to be so. There is a provision in scripture for a lasting solution. The scriptures says in Jeremiah 31: 29-30, "In those days they shall say no more, they Fathers have eaten a sour grape, and the children's teeth are set on edge. But everyone shall die for his own iniquity: Every man that eateth the sour grape, his teeth shall be set on edge".

To help your children walk through the minefield of repercussions capable of arising from the evil foundations we inherited from our fore bears, I suggest you do thorough job of sorting out your family's foundation by undertaking the following steps;

1.   Repent of your sins and cry out to God for help. 1John1:8-10

2.   Accept Jesus Christ as your personal Lord and Savior and lead your children to the Lord...Acts 2:38

3.   Research into your family foundations and take note of the things that have happened repeatedly. Reflect on your ways where have you been and what things have you done in the past? Did you marry your spouse properly before you had your children? Did you go anywhere to pray to have children after your marriage? I ask these questions because some people go to Juju priest, mermaid, palm readers and water spirits to make supplication for children. Others just co-habit and carry on relationships for convenience sake. They do not properly marry or have any serious commitment to each other. They may change sexual partners regularly and start having children without proper marriage. If you did this then you need to repent and go for deliverance ministration. Rectify your illegal union and build on a reinforced foundation.

4.   Take stock of happenings in your family. Have you experienced untimely death, miscarriages, sudden disappearance of people, tragedies that are inexplicable? Look at the names your family bears. Is it a good name? Can that name attract a blessing from GOD? Trace the meaning and the roots of the name. Where did the name

come from? Are your children named after a god of thunder, a mountain deity, river goddess, a juju priest or an old wicked relation?

5. Trace your family history to know your descendants. Do you know exactly what your family name means? Do you know the origins of your family? Are there any hidden things in the family that family members are ashamed to talk about openly? These include such things as cases of murder, insanity and wickedness? What about the names given to your children? Are they honorable names? Change any name that will not attract God's Favor. Replace such names with useful, God honoring and blessing and attracting names. The names that people bear not only define their character, these names also affect the fulfillment of the people's destiny. In Chronicles 4: 9-10 we read how God brought Jabez out of obscurity. This is why God changed the names of several people in the Bible. For your personal study you can look up the following examples:

a. Abram: In Genesis 17:5 God Changed Abram's name to "Abraham", meaning the "father of many nations".

b. Sarai –her name was changed to Sareh. Genesis 17:15

c. Jacob – His name was changed to Israel. Genesis 32:26-29.

In Genesis 35:10 the word of God says that after Jacob returned from Paddam Aram, God appeared to him again and blessed him. God said to him, "your name is Jacob, but you will be Israel. When God Changes your name and gives you a new name, he becomes jealous over you and keeps you as the apple of his eyes. Jacob himself changed the name that Rachel, his wife gave to his last child. Rachel called the baby "Ben-oni" which means "Son of my trouble", But Jacob renamed the child "Benjamin" meaning "Son of my right hand" Genesis 35:16-18.

d.   Saul – after his encounter with Jesus on the way to Damascus his name changed to Raul. See Acts 9:1-22

As you will notice from these scriptures, a wrong name can actually delay one's blessing as in the case of Jacob or prevent the bearer from ever getting to the place of rest and enlargement. Therefore, do yourself and your children a favor. Ask God to reveal that which needs to be rectified about your family foundations. Do a careful study of your own name and the names of your children. You have no business bearing a name that is a dedication to demons or idols. Did any of your family raise strange alters(shrines) for evil purposes. Check this out very carefully. Confess very exhaustively each of your own sins and identificational repentance for the sins of your children and ancestors. This is what Nehemiah did. Study the methodical way that Nehemiah went about confessing the sins of his family and the sins of the Jews as a community. Nehemiah 1:4-8. A list of sins you can begin to confess to God include the following:

a.   Idolatry – Exodus 20:1-4, God hates idolatry and will always punish idol worshippers. Read Jeremiah 44:L 3-13; Deut. 13:1-11

b.   Murder and other forms of blood guiltiness, 2 Sam 21:1-5, deut. 21:1-9, Exodus 20: 13, Proverbs 28:17 says "A man burdened with bloodshed will flee into a pit, let no one help

c.   Sexual sins such as adultery (Exodus 20:14) and fornication(I Corinth, 6:18, gen. 38: 1-30, 2 Sam.11: 2-5: Incest, (Lex. 18:6-18) Bestiality(having sex with animals) (lex. 18:23-24). If you ever have been involved in many of these sins then take a step in the right direction. Repent and cry out to God for help. It is an abomination that attracts curses. Juday committed fornication and incest with his widowed daughter-in-law and for this reason hisline lost the inheritance.

d.   Lying, deceit, backbiting, anger, stealing, (Exodus 20: 15-17); drunkenness and witchcraft are other sins you should repent of when you have identified that you are standing on an evil foundation, settle down to reflect on how God wants you to tackle the situation. First, realize that God forgives sins. The Bible records in Isaiah 1:18 "Come now, and let us reason together, saith the Lord: Though your sins be as scarlet they shall be as white as snow; though they shall be red as crimson, they shall be as wool." Genuine deliverance: Follow the example of Nehemiah and Ezra. Take a fast and pray. (Ezra 8:21). Mourn, weep, ask the Lord to forgive you and your children.

Refer to Daniel's Prayer for his people as recorded in Daniel 9:3-19. It is a good example of the kind of supplication you need to bring before the Lord.

Declare that God is righteous and that his judgments are well deserved. Ask that He forgive you and your family only because of his mercy and the work of redemption that Jesus wrought on the cross.

a.   Repeat of every known sin, calling each sin by name.

b.   Renounce the sin and turn from it.

c.   Identify and break the curses that are associated with those sins that had bound you Previously. Nullify every curse and sanction from evil powers by the blood of Jesus. Hebrews 9:11-15.

d.   Your freed from the powers that bound you to these sins. Psalms 19: 12-13

e.   Declare that the hold of these sins is broken over your life and the lives of your children.

Ask the Lord to heal you and your children permanently. Hosea 6: 1-2 says, "Come, and let us return unto the LORD: For he hath tom, and he will heal us: he hath smitten, and he will bind us up". After two days will he revive us in the third day he will raise us up, and we shall live in his sight.

f.   Ask that the blood of Jesus would speak freedom, mercy, cleansing and refreshing in your lives.

g.   Charge everything in creation the heavens, the earth, the sun, moon and stars, the mountains and hills – to bear witness to the fact that you have built a new alter unto God for your family. Seal this new covenant with the blood of Jesus.

You have to do this because certain things that children suffer comes as a result of the things that their parents do.

Also, there are certain habits, tragedies, reproaches and outright sins that are traceable to generational sins. And generational sins bring generational consequences. Now let us look briefly at some generational sins in order to discover what we must do to gain freedom permanently.

a. Dishonoring parents: In Genesis 9:22, Ham, one of the sons of Noah saw his father's nakedness. Instead of looking for a robe to cover his father's naked body, Ham mocked at his father who had fallen into a drunken stupor and this earned his descendants a curse up till this day. Noah was so offended by his son's action that he spoke without thinking. Naturally we would prefer for Ham to have been given the punishment for his action and not his children. "And he said, Cursed be Canaan; a servant of servants shall he be unto his brethren." Gen. 9:25. The point we must note is that both Noah and Ham had sinned. Noah had taken too much Wine and he lay naked in his tent. Ham on the other hand, sinned because he mocked at his father. He should have done what his two brothers did. "And Shem and Japheth took a garment, and laid it upon both their shoulders, and went backward, and covered the nakedness of their Father; and their faces were backward, and they saw not their father's nakedness" Gen (:23. Note that the curse for Ham's sins came upon his descendants. Do you want your children to suffer from the curses that your own sins attract? Disrespecting elders also attract punishment from God. 1 Timothy 5:1 says, "rebuke not an elder, but entreat him as a Father. In II Kings 2:23-24 the issue of showing disrespect to elder------a prophet of God sent 42 children to an untimely grave. And he went up from thence unto Bethel: and as he was going up by the way, there came forth little children out of the City and mocked him, and said unto him, Go up, thou bald head: go up, thou bald head.

And he turned back, and looked on them, and cursed them in the name of the LORD. And there came forth two she bears out of the wood, and are forty and two_children of them.

b.   Greed and deceit. In 2 Kings 5:21-23, Gehazi, the servant of Elisha sinned a great sin. He deceived Namaan, the captain of the Syrian army and obtained gifts that his master did not ask him to collect. When asked what he had done he lied to Elisha. For this reason Elisha pronounced a curse on his generations. Said the prophet "The leprosy therefore of Naaman shall Cleave unto thee, and unto they seed forever. And he went out from his presence a leper as white as snow." 2 Kings 5:27.

c.   Immorality and Sexual sins. In 2 Samuel 1:2-5, David was ensnared by lust and he committed adultery with Bathshebad Uriah's wife. To cover up his sin he killed Uriah the Hittite by asking Joab, the army commander, to send him to the front lines where the battle was very fierce. God punished David and pronounced judgment on his house. The LORD said to David, through Prophet Nathan,: Now therefore the sword shall ever depart from thine house; because thou has despised me, and hasttaken the wife of Uriah the Hittite to be thy wife. Thus saith the LORD, Behold, I will raise up evil against thee out of thine own house, and I will take thy wives before thine eyes, and give them unto neighbor, and he shall lie with thy wives in the sight of this sun. For "Thou didst it secretly: but I will do this thing before the sun. "2 Samuel 12:10-12.

Note that God's word came to pass in David's family when Ahithopel advised Absalom to dishonor his father's bed by openly having sex with his Father's Concubines at the housetop. (2 Samuel 16:21-22). This was the most abhorrent thing that a son could do in Isreal. In addition Amnon raped Tamar, Absalom's sister. (2 Samuel 13: 10-19). As a result of this sin, Absalom plotted the murder of Amnon. (2 Samuel 13:28-29). Absalom himself later died by the sword. 2 Samuel 18:9-14.

A Point of Ponder. Drop this book for a moment and ponder over the words you have just read. This sin of the Father can still affect the children except where there is someone to stand in the gap and plead for the forgiveness of these sins.

Intercede for your family. What does it mean to "Stand in the gap for your family'? Ezekel 22:30 says "And I sought for a man among them that should make up the hedge, and stand in the gap before me for the land, that I should not destroy it: But I found none." When you begin to intercede fervently for your children, you break Satan's power to rule over them using generational sins. On the other hand if you refuse to intercede then your children will be punished. Ezekiel 22:31 shows what happen when there is no intercessor for family. "Therefore have I poured out mine indignation upon them; I have consumed them with the fire of my urath: their own way have I recompensed upon their heads, said the Lord God.

d.   Adultery. God hates the sin of idolatry. That is why He gave it as the first commandment. See Exodus 20:3-5. In 2 Kings 9:3-10, God raised Jehu to judge the house of Ahab, the Idolatrous King of Isreal because of the sins that he and his wife(Jezebel) had committed. Although Ahab repented, and the sentence was deferred, the axe fell on his children. Please let the examples we have looked at instruct you. Make a detailed list of your sins and the Sins of your children.

HOW TO DEAL WITH GENERATIONALSINS

1. Repent over them very thoroughly by confessing the sins out loud to God. Forsake the sins one after the other. Please don't cover up anything. Cry to God to forgive and show mercy because we cannot prosper if we cover our sins.

2. Make atonement by the blood of Jesus Christ. Colossians 1:20-21

3. Speak prophetically calling forth healing in the name of Jesus. Isaiah 53:5

4. Pray and dedicate one bottle of anointing oil,(olive oil). Then use it to anoint your head and the heads of your children. Renounce each sin and its effect. Break the tokens of the covenants your family may have entered into with Satan. Present your children as a ramsome unto the Lord.

5. Burn any token that represent the old covenant. This could a piece of cloth, a document, a ring or a symbol like cowry shells or manila. Destroy all those things and sack the priests that used to service those alters. Dry up their anointing and declare that they no more speak or act on your behalf.

6.   Raise a new alter unto God for your family. Name this alter in the same way that Gideon gave a specific name to the alter he built for the Lord in Judges 6:24.

7.   Call upon the Lord to fight for your family and defend you from this alter. Cry to the Lord night and day calling on him to help your children.

8.   Ask that God would release angles to man the alter.

9.   Ask God to heal your family and give you help if you address the issues we have been discussing in this chapter in all honesty and sincerity. God has promised to help you. "if my people, which are called by my name, shall humble themselves, and pray, and seek my face, and turn from their wicked ways, then will I hear from heaven, and will forgive their sins, and will heal their land." 2 chron. 7:14.

CHAPTER 7

BE ENCOURAGED, YOUR LABOR WILL BE REWARED

In this last chapter, we bring all sincere and committed parents a word from the Lord. It is a word of encouragement and hope.

Thus said the LORD; A voice was heard in Romah, Lamentation, and bitter weeping for her children refused to be comforted for her children, because they were not.

Thus saith the LORD; Refram thy voice from weeping and thy eyes from tears for thy work shall be rewarded, saith the LORD; and they shall come again from the land of the enemy. Jermiah 31:15-16.

God would want me to remind you that your labors in training children for the Lord will be rewarded. Note that you have a duty to Jesus Christ and disciple them to live for Christ. The bible says: "the rod and reproof give wisdom: but a child left to himself bringeth his mother to shame Prov. 29:15.

Correct the son and he shall give thee rest: yea, he shall give delight unto thy soul.

There is a generation that cureth their father, and doth not bless their mother.

There is a generation that is pure in their own eye, and yet is not washed from their filthiness. Proverbs 30: 11:12.

Realize that as you train your children as a faithful steward, you are blessed now and you will be doubly blessed and honored in your old Age. When all your children become useful adults you will be very glad indeed. You will know the venture was well worth the trouble. Your name will be remembered and your children will grow to become mighty men in the Land. They shall spread like the cedars of Lebanon.

Never forget this "…..A wise son maketh a glad Father: But a foolish son is heaviness of his mother."

Be Strong in the Lord and in the power of his night. Train the children as unto the Lord. Encourage yourself with the words of Psalm 128:1-4. "Blessed is everyone that feareth the LORD that walked in his ways.
For thou shalt eat the Labor of thine hands: happy shalt thou be, and it shall be well with thee.
Thy wife shall be as a fruitful vine by the sides of thine house thy children like olive plants round about thy table. Behold, that thus shall the man be blessed that feared the

LORD. Col. 3:23-24 and whatsoever ye do, do it heartily, as to the Lord and not unto men, knowing that of the Lord ye shall receive the reward of inheritance for ye serve the Lord Christ. God has entrusted into your hands all the children you have. He wants you to train them for him and care for them as a faithful steward. At the appointed time the LORD of the harvest will reward you.

CHAPTER 8

SCRPTURES TO HELP PARENTS IN MATTERS CONCERNING CHILDREN

1. Children as gifts/blessing from God.   Gen. 33:5
   Prove 10:1 Do you gladden your Father's heart?

   Psalm 127: 3-5, Psalm 128:3-4

2. Where to find help to correct your children
   Prov. 13:24 Don't spare the rod
   Prov. 19:18 Chasten your children
   Prov. 22:15 Discipline them in love
   Prov. 29:15 Don't leave your children to their own devices.
   Proverbs 29:15 Correct your son and he will give you rest.

3. God's commandment to children.
   Exodus 20:12 Honor your Parents
   Exodus 21:15 Never you strike/beat your parents

Lev. 19:3 Respect your Parents
Psalm 119:9 Take head to God's word
Eph. 6:1-3 Obey and honor your parents
2 Timonthy 5:1 Don't rebuke an elder
Prov. 17:6 Are you a crown to your grandparents

4. Instruction to parents to teach children
Deut. 6: 6-9 Device ingenious way to reach/teach your children
God's ordinances
Psalm 78:8 Don't hide God's word from your children
Prov. 22:6 Show them the way
Prov. 31:1-4 Instruct your children in righteousness.
Prov. 31:1 Teach your children prophecies.

5. God's Commandment to Parents
Ephesians 6:4 - Don't provoke them
Proverbs 22:6 - Train them in God's way
1 Timothy 5:8 - Provide for them
Proverbs 29:15 and Proverbs 22:15 - Discipline them so they won't bring you shame
Proverbs 17:21 – Ensure that your children do not become fools.

Repent from sin – "Except ye repent ye shall likewise perish". Luke 13:3. "Repent ye therefore, and be converted that your sins maybe blotted out….." Acts 3:19
Forsake Sin – "Let the wicked forsake his ways, and the unrighteous man his thoughts and let him return unto the Lord, and He will have mercy upon him, and to our God,

for He will abundantly pardon" – Isaiah 55:7.

Believe Jesus – "He that believeth and is baptized not shall be dammed Mark 16:16.
Receive Jesus – " He came unto His own, and his own received Him not. But as many as received Him, to them He gave the right to become children of God, even to them that believed on his name." John 1: 11-12
Abide in Jesus – " Abide in Jesus(me) and I in you. As the branch cannot bear fruit of itself, except it abide in the vine; no more can ye, except ye abide in me." – John 15-4

Other Books by Bishop Dr. Godfrey K. Tabansi are Available Now for Purchase

1. Hitting The Target in Soul Winning

2. By Prayer and Fasting

For any information, comments and/or if you would like to reach Bishop Tabansi, please contact us at:

Divine Publishers Inc.
www.divinepublishersinc.com
Email: divinepublishersinc@gmail.com

www.ingramcontent.com/pod-product-compliance
Lightning Source LLC
Chambersburg PA
CBHW061250040426
42444CB00010B/2339